CW00403135

SPIRIT OF THE

SEVERN VALLEY
RAILWAY

MIKE HEATH

First published in Great Britain in 2009

Copyright text and photographs © 2009 Mike Heath

British Library Cataloguing-in-Publication Data
A CIP record for this title is available from the British Library

ISBN 978 1 906887 39 1

PiXZ Books
Halsgrove House, Ryelands Industrial Estate,
Bagley Road, Wellington, Somerset TA21 9PZ
Tel: 01823 653777
Fax: 01823 216796
email: sales@halsgrove.com

An imprint of Halstar Ltd, part of the Halsgrove group of companies
Information on all Halsgrove titles is available at: www.halsgrove.com

Printed and bound by Grafiche Flaminia, Italy

Introduction

The Severn Valley Railway of today follows the meandering course of the River Severn from the Shropshire town of Bridgnorth in the north, through the villages of Hampton Loade, Highley, and Arley to the Worcestershire town of Bewdley, where it leaves the river and heads east to terminate in Kidderminster.

The line is a major tourist attraction and the journey along it is fascinating, passing as it does through varied and mostly unspoilt landscapes between a number of beautifully restored country stations each of which retains its own unique timeless charm. The scenery on offer is only really available to rail passengers, walkers (and photographers) as there is limited road access to the area.

The massive storms in 2007 devastated the railway which suffered damage in 45 separate locations. However, with finance raised from every source, be it individual donations or large funding organisations combined with a massive human effort, the nightmare turned into a dream with the railway reopening in March 2008. Add to this the long awaited opening of the Visitors Centre at Highley and the 'line for all seasons' was back in business.

Bridgnorth Station, a listed building, was first opened in 1862 and became the birthplace of the preserved Severn Valley Railway in 1965.

Former Great Western Pannier Tank No. 7714, in British Railway guise, heads south into an autumnal tinted landscape in October 1994.

On 7 March 2009 Great Western Railway 2-6-2T No. 5164 climbs away from Bridgnorth with a morning train.

Having crossed over the Bridgnorth By-Pass 'small Prairie' GWR 2-6-2T No. 4566 powers through Oldbury Cutting back in February 2007.

Emerging from the cutting during the 2009 Festival of Steam is a pristine 'Erlestoke Manor' sporting a 'Pembroke Coast Express' headboard.

A special visitor at the 'Festival', held over the weekend 6, 7 & 8 March 2009,
was the unique British Railways Standard Class 8P No. 71000 'Duke of Gloucester'.

Crossing the five arch Oldbury Viaduct, during a charter on 29 September 2008, is visiting GWR Prairie No. 5526 complete with auto-coach. Both are normally based on the South Devon Railway at Buckfastleigh.

Having just passed the line's summit at Eardington trains ease off as a private track is crossed.

Above:
The crossing cottage housed the Keeper who looked after the crossing
gates and worked at Eardington a cycle ride down the track.

Right:
On a cold and frosty 3 January 2009 morning former LMS 2-6-0 No. 42968 bursts
out of the mist as it nears the summit of Eardington Bank with a Bridgnorth-bound train.
Photo: Karl Heath

Eardington Bank is a favourite location for photographers, as northbound locomotives work hard tackling the gradient. During the 2009 'Festival' 'Duke of Gloucester' did however take it in its stride.

14

On 19 November 2004 a late afternoon 'local' in the
hands of No. 5164 takes it at a more leisurely pace.

Eardington Halt is located at some distance from its village and was built to serve two ironworks. It is now used as a Permanent Way depot. Back in 1997 BR Standard 2-6-4T No. 80079 was viewed passing through with a pick-up goods train. Next stop Hampton Loade. This locomotive is currently stored out of service in the Engine House exhibition hall at Highley.

Passing Hay Bridge at the head of the railway's LNER teak stock on 14 November 2004 is GWR Pannier Tank No. 7714, in Great Western livery. This is another location where as a photographer you are unlikely to be alone. Just south of here is Sterns, the location of a landslide that has resulted in a speed restriction for all trains.

Above:
With a 1 in 100 gradient to ascend shortly after,
locomotives have to work hard as they accelerate away.

Right:
Glinting in the afternoon sunshine is LMS Ivatt
Class 2-6-0 No. 46443.

Just south of Hampton Loade the line passes through an open part of the valley with trees lining the opposite river bank providing a colourful backdrop in late summer.

Even in winter there's no denying the country railway charm of the line.

Left:
When steam services from Bridgnorth restarted in 1970, Hampton Loade was the southern terminus for passenger services. A footplate experience train in the hands of No. 42968 starts back towards Bridgnorth on a bright October 2008 morning.

Right:
The station is in a time-warp with its period lighting and posters by day . . .

. . . and the irresistible warmth of a coal fire in the
welcoming waiting room at night. (Photo Karl Heath)

On 14 November 2004 No. 7714 eases
out of the station on its way to the northern terminus.

Heading south piloting 'Erlestoke Manor' is the Bluebell Railway's GWR Dukedog No. 9017 which was a very welcome and popular visitor in 2008.

In its previous life Highley Station was the hub of a colliery district serving up to four local mines. Thankfully it has been meticulously restored. At the time of writing work was underway to erect a footbridge over the running lines to take the place of the boarded crossing in the foreground. This will allow passengers to cross the line safely on their way to visit the new Engine House exhibition centre.

Highley is a great place to take a break from travelling to watch the railway in action as the footplate crew exchange tokens with the signalman . . .

. . . and on enthusiast weekends the sidings can be full of trains awaiting permission to continue their journeys. This photo was taken at the 2000 Spring Gala. It is worth noting that Highley suffered greatly as a result of the floods in 2007 with a large section of track, water tower and cattle dock washed into the valley.

Taking pride of place in the exhibition centre are locomotives currently out of service awaiting their turn in the workshop's restoration programme. A number of the photographs in this album were taken during charters organised by the 'Friends of the locomotive Hagley Hall' to raise funds for the eagerly awaited restoration of No. 4930.

The locomotive currently mothballed alongside 'Hagley Hall' in the Engine House is standard heavy freight, 8F, 2-8-0 locomotive No. 48773. Seen here many years earlier, in August 2003 with an afternoon departure from Highley.

There is a clear view of the sweep of track south of the station from the front of the Engine House.

Arley is one of the most attractive stations on the line serving the village of Upper Arley on the opposite river bank. It dates from the opening of the line in 1862.

At peak times trains are timetabled to cross here, and additional enthusiast weekend 'locals' terminate here making it the busiest country station on the line.

A short walk along the river bank is the largest engineering structure on the line, Victoria Bridge. A 2005 Autumn Gala Weekend freight crosses, hauled by a visitor from the North Yorkshire Moors Railway, ex-GWR 0-6-2T No. 6619. (Karl Heath)

When built, in 1861, the bridge's single span of 200 feet was the longest in the world.

With all trains slowing to cross the bridge there is ample time to take photographs. LMS No. 42968 was captured on film on 15 March 2003. It is also a very peaceful location to spend time between trains. It is here that I saw my first Kingfisher flitting about the riverbank.

Above:
Water abstracted from the Severn at a regulated rate is stored in Trimpley Reservoirs for use at times of peak demand when it is fed into the Elan Aqueduct to supplement Birmingham's water supply.

Right:
Having just passed Northwood Halt, No. 46443 is whistling a warning on the approach to a farm crossing during the 1997 Spring Gala.

On the outskirts of Bewdley the Midland Railway Centre's Standard 2-6-4T No. 80080 passes the point where the former branch to Tenbury Wells would have emerged from the left to run alongside the Severn Valley line for the last mile to Bewdley. The locomotive was a visitor for the Autumn Gala in 1999.

At that same gala Heavy Freight 2-8-0T No. 4277 pounds out of Bewdley with a Bridgnorth-bound train. The sloping track bed of the branch can be seen in the foreground.

Left:
No. 42968 passes the same location but fails to attract the attention of a fisherman.

Right:
On 3 January 2009 much of the southern section of the railway was covered by freezing fog (see page 13). Around Bewdley the mist drifted around leaving a hoar-frost on the trees.

Left:
Note the absence of
fishermen in these
conditions!

Right:
That same day
'Erlestoke Manor' was
photographed across
the medieval rooftops
of Bewdley with
an afternoon
post-Christmas train.

The locomotive's owning group, 'The Erlstoke Manor Fund', organised a photography charter on 10 October 2008 and the last shots of that day were of the 'Manor' hauling freight stock across Wribbenhall Viaduct on the approach to Bewdley Station.

A general view of platform 1 looking north on the morning of another charter. This one organised by the 'Hagley Hall' locomotive supporting group on 29 September 2008.

A working member of the group is playing a starring role in this atmospheric image.

During an organised night shoot in February 2007 No. 4566 was posed alongside the North signal box completing a wonderfully timeless scene.

Above:
It was equally impressive alongside Platform 1 a little later that evening.

Right:
On an October night in 2001 Black Five No. 45110
posed in Platform 2 with a Night Mail train.

Left:
The splendid array of signals around Bewdley South signal box is testimony to the excellent work of the railway's Signal and Telecommunications Department. The safe operation of the railway depends on them.

Right:
A vintage recreation of a Great Western Railway scene with Dukedog 'Earl of Berkeley' at the head of a rake of beautifully restored goods wagons on 10 October 2008.

Just south of Bewdley the railway passes along an embankment which overlooks the West Midlands Safari Park giving passengers glimpses of world wild life roaming the grounds.

Visiting locomotives are a main attraction at Enthusiast Weekends and one notable example is former Somerset and Dorset Railway 2-8-0 No. 88 which has been restored in a striking Prussian blue livery by the S&DR Trust at their base on the West Somerset Railway. This image was taken during its March 2007 visit.

Another feature of gala weekends is the running of freight trains between passenger services recreating images from the 1950s. No. 46443 cruises down towards Bewdley on 15 March 2003.

During that same Spring Gala a vintage train is seen heading for Kidderminster. The locomotive is Taff Vale Railway 0-6-2 tank No. 85 which dates from 1899 when it was built to haul coal trains in South Wales. Its preservation home is the Keighley & Worth Valley Railway in West Yorkshire.

Memories of the Cambrian Coast Railway were stirred when the visiting Dukedog was paired with 'Erlestoke Manor' on a passenger train as part of the 10 October 2008 charter.

Later that afternoon the 'Manor' took charge of what was
thought to be one of its first freight trains in preservation.

This location is
known as Rifle
Range and a halt of
that name was open
from 1905 to 1920
for the use of
Yeomanry
volunteers training
on the adjacent
heathland.

On 19 October 2001 Black Five No. 45110 emerges from the 480 yards long Bewdley Tunnel into the sun-blessed heathland with a northbound train.

On the outskirts of Kidderminster is Falling Sands Viaduct which carries the railway over both the River Stour and the Staffordshire and Worcestershire Canal.

This splendid signal gantry controls all access to Kidderminster Station.

Kidderminster Town Station was built from new on the site of the former British Rail goods yard alongside the main rail network's own station. Participants in a 'Friends of the locomotive Hagley Hall' charter partake of lunch during a break in a thoroughly enjoyable day of steam photography.